I0482967

This informational booklet is
intended to provide a generic,
non-exhaustive overview of a
particular standards-related topic.
This publication does not itself
alter or determine compliance
responsibilities, which are set
forth in OSHA standards themselves
and the *Occupational
Safety and Health Act*. Moreover,
because interpretations and
enforcement policy may change
over time, for additional guidance
on OSHA compliance requirements,
the reader should consult
current and administrative
interpretations and decisions by
the Occupational Safety and
Health Review Commission
and the courts.

Material contained in this
publication is in the public domain
and may be reproduced, fully or
partially, without permission of the
Federal Government. Source credit is
requested but not required.

This information will be made
available to sensory impaired
individuals upon request.

Voice phone: (202) 693-1999

Hand and Power Tools

U.S. Department of Labor
Elaine L. Chao, Secretary

Occupational Safety and Health Administration
John L. Henshaw, Assistant Secretary

OSHA 3080
2002 (Revised)

What Is the Purpose of This Booklet? 1

What Are the Hazards of Hand Tools? 3

What Are the Dangers of Power Tools? 4
  Guards 5
  Operating Controls and Switches 5
  Electric Tools 6
  Portable Abrasive Wheel Tools 7
  Pneumatic Tools 8
  Liquid Fuel Tools 9
  Powder-Actuated Tools 9
  Hydraulic Power Tools 11

What Help Can OSHA Provide? 13
  Safety and Health Program Management Guidelines 13
  State Programs 13
  Consultation Services 14
  Voluntary Protection Programs 15
  Strategic Partnership Program 15
  Training and Education 15
  Electronic Information 16
  OSHA Publications 17
  Emergencies, Complaints, and Further Assistance.... 18

States and Territories with Approved Plans 19

OSHA Consultation Project Directory 22

OSHA Area Offices 24

OSHA Regional Offices 27

This booklet is designed to present to employees and employers a summary of the basic safety procedures and safeguards associated with hand and portable power tools.

Material in this booklet is based on the standards of the Occupational Safety and Health Administration; this booklet, however, should not be considered as a substitute for the full safety and health standards for general industry (published in Title 29 *Code of Federal Regulations* (CFR), Part 1910, Subpart P), or for the construction industry (published in *29 CFR* Part 1926, Subpart I). These are also available on the World Wide Web at www.osha.gov.

Employers and employees in the 26 states and territories with OSHA-approved state safety and health plans should check with their state agency. Their state may be enforcing standards and other procedures that, while "at least as effective as" federal standards, are not always identical to the federal requirements. (See page 13 for more information on state plans.)

Tools are such a common part of our lives that it is difficult to remember that they may pose hazards. Tragically, a serious incident can occur before steps are taken to identify and avoid or eliminate tool-related hazards.

Employees who use hand and power tools and are exposed to the hazards of falling, flying, abrasive, and splashing objects, or to harmful dusts, fumes, mists, vapors, or gases must be provided with the appropriate personal protective equipment. All electrical connections for these tools must be suitable for the type of tool and the working conditions (wet, dusty, flammable vapors). When a temporary power source is used for construction a ground-fault circuit interrupter should be used.

Employees should be trained in the proper use of all tools. Workers should be able to recognize the hazards associated with the different types of tools and the safety precautions necessary.

Five basic safety rules can help prevent hazards associated with the use of hand and power tools:

- Keep all tools in good condition with regular maintenance.
- Use the right tool for the job.
- Examine each tool for damage before use and do not use damaged tools.
- Operate tools according to the manufacturers' instructions.

- Provide and use properly the right personal protective equipment.

Employees and employers should work together to establish safe working procedures. If a hazardous situation is encountered, it should be brought immediately to the attention of the proper individual for hazard abatement.

The following sections identify various types of hand and power tools and their potential hazards. They also identify ways to prevent worker injury through proper use of the tools and through the use of appropriate personal protective equipment.

Hand tools are tools that are powered manually. Hand tools include anything from axes to wrenches. The greatest hazards posed by hand tools result from misuse and improper maintenance.

Some examples include the following:

- If a chisel is used as a screwdriver, the tip of the chisel may break and fly off, hitting the user or other employees.
- If a wooden handle on a tool, such as a hammer or an axe, is loose, splintered, or cracked, the head of the tool may fly off and strike the user or other employees.
- If the jaws of a wrench are sprung, the wrench might slip.
- If impact tools such as chisels, wedges, or drift pins have mushroomed heads, the heads might shatter on impact, sending sharp fragments flying toward the user or other employees.

The employer is responsible for the safe condition of tools and equipment used by employees. Employers shall not issue or permit the use of unsafe hand tools. Employees should be trained in the proper use and handling of tools and equipment.

Employees, when using saw blades, knives, or other tools, should direct the tools away from aisle areas and away from other employees working in close proximity. Knives and scissors must be sharp; dull tools can cause more hazards than sharp ones. Cracked saw blades must be removed from service.

Wrenches must not be used when jaws are sprung to the point that slippage occurs. Impact tools such as drift pins, wedges, and chisels must be kept free of mushroomed heads. The wooden handles of tools must not be splintered.

Iron or steel hand tools may produce sparks that can be an ignition source around flammable substances. Where this hazard exists, spark-resistant tools made of non-ferrous materials should be used where flammable gases, highly volatile liquids, and other explosive substances are stored or used.

Appropriate personal protective equipment such as safety goggles and gloves must be worn to protect against hazards that may be encountered while using hand tools.

Workplace floors shall be kept as clean and dry as possible to prevent accidental slips with or around dangerous hand tools.

Power tools must be fitted with guards and safety switches; they are extremely hazardous when used improperly. The types of power tools are determined by their power source: electric, pneumatic, liquid fuel, hydraulic, and powder-actuated.

To prevent hazards associated with the use of power tools, workers should observe the following general precautions:

- Never carry a tool by the cord or hose.
- Never yank the cord or the hose to disconnect it from the receptacle.
- Keep cords and hoses away from heat, oil, and sharp edges.
- Disconnect tools when not using them, before servicing and cleaning them, and when changing accessories such as blades, bits, and cutters.
- Keep all people not involved with the work at a safe distance from the work area.
- Secure work with clamps or a vise, freeing both hands to operate the tool.
- Avoid accidental starting. Do not hold fingers on the switch button while carrying a plugged-in tool.
- Maintain tools with care; keep them sharp and clean for best performance.
- Follow instructions in the user's manual for lubricating and changing accessories.
- Be sure to keep good footing and maintain good balance when operating power tools.
- Wear proper apparel for the task. Loose clothing, ties, or jewelry can become caught in moving parts.
- Remove all damaged portable electric tools from use and tag them: "Do Not Use."

Guards

The exposed moving parts of power tools need to be safe-guarded. Belts, gears, shafts, pulleys, sprockets, spindles, drums, flywheels, chains, or other reciprocating, rotating, or moving parts of equipment must be guarded.

Machine guards, as appropriate, must be provided to protect the operator and others from the following:

- Point of operation.
- In-running nip points.
- Rotating parts.
- Flying chips and sparks.

Safety guards must never be removed when a tool is being used. Portable circular saws having a blade greater than 2 inches (5.08 centimeters) in diameter must be equipped at all times with guards. An upper guard must cover the entire blade of the saw. A retract-able lower guard must cover the teeth of the saw, except where it makes contact with the work material. The lower guard must automatically return to the covering position when the tool is withdrawn from the work material.

Operating Controls and Switches

The following hand-held power tools must be equipped with a constant-pressure switch or control that shuts off the power when pressure is released: drills; tappers; fastener drivers; horizontal, vertical, and angle grinders with wheels more than 2 inches (5.08 centimeters) in diameter; disc sanders with discs greater than 2 inches (5.08 centimeters); belt sanders; reciprocating saws; saber saws, scroll saws, and jigsaws with blade shanks greater than $1/4$-inch (0.63 centimeters) wide; and other similar tools. These tools also may be equipped with a "lock-on" control, if it allows the worker to also shut off the control in a single motion using the same finger or fingers. The following hand-held power tools must be equipped with either a positive "on-off" control switch, a constant pressure switch, or a "lock-on" control: disc sanders with discs 2 inches (5.08 centi-meters) or less in diameter; grinders with wheels 2 inches (5.08 centimeters) or less in diameter; platen sanders, routers, planers, laminate trimmers, nibblers, shears, and scroll saws; and jigsaws, saber and scroll saws with blade shanks a nominal $1/4$-inch (6.35 millimeters) or less in diameter. It is recommended that the constant-pressure control switch be regarded as the preferred device.

Other hand-held power tools such as circular saws having a blade diameter greater than 2 inches (5.08 centimeters), chain saws, and percussion tools with no means of holding accessories securely must be equipped with a constant-pressure switch.

Electric Tools

Employees using electric tools must be aware of several dangers. Among the most serious hazards are electrical burns and shocks.

Electrical shocks, which can lead to injuries such as heart failure and burns, are among the major hazards associated with electric-powered tools. Under certain conditions, even a small amount of electric current can result in fibrillation of the heart and death. An electric shock also can cause the user to fall off a ladder or other elevated work surface and be injured due to the fall.

To protect the user from shock and burns, electric tools must have a three-wire cord with a ground and be plugged into a grounded receptacle, be double insulated, or be powered by a low-voltage isolation transformer. Three-wire cords contain two current-carrying conductors and a grounding conductor. Any time an adapter is used to accommodate a two-hole receptacle, the adapter wire must be attached to a known ground. The third prong must never be removed from the plug.

Double-insulated tools are available that provide protection against electrical shock without third-wire grounding. On double-insulated tools, an internal layer of protective insulation completely isolates the external housing of the tool.

The following general practices should be followed when using electric tools:

- Operate electric tools within their design limitations.
- Use gloves and appropriate safety footwear when using electric tools.
- Store electric tools in a dry place when not in use.

- Do not use electric tools in damp or wet locations unless they are approved for that purpose.
- Keep work areas well lighted when operating electric tools.
- Ensure that cords from electric tools do not present a tripping hazard.

In the construction industry, employees who use electric tools must be protected by ground-fault circuit interrupters or an assured equipment-grounding conductor program.

Portable Abrasive Wheel Tools

Portable abrasive grinding, cutting, polishing, and wire buffing wheels create special safety problems because they may throw off flying fragments. Abrasive wheel tools must be equipped with guards that: (1) cover the spindle end, nut, and flange projections; (2) maintain proper alignment with the wheel; and (3) do not exceed the strength of the fastenings.

Before an abrasive wheel is mounted, it must be inspected closely for damage and should be sound- or ring-tested to ensure that it is free from cracks or defects. To test, wheels should be tapped gently with a light, non-metallic instrument. If the wheels sound cracked or dead, they must not be used because they could fly apart in operation. A stable and undamaged wheel, when tapped, will give a clear metallic tone or "ring."

To prevent an abrasive wheel from cracking, it must fit freely on the spindle. The spindle nut must be tightened enough to hold the wheel in place without distorting the flange. Always follow the manufacturer's recommendations. Take care to ensure that the spindle speed of the machine will not exceed the maximum operating speed marked on the wheel.

An abrasive wheel may disintegrate or explode during start-up. Allow the tool to come up to operating speed prior to grinding or cutting. The employee should never stand in the plane of rotation of the wheel as it accelerates to full operating speed. Portable grinding tools need to be equipped with safety guards to protect workers not only from the moving wheel surface, but also from flying fragments in case of wheel breakage.

When using a powered grinder:
- Always use eye or face protection.
- Turn off the power when not in use.
- Never clamp a hand-held grinder in a vise.

Pneumatic Tools

Pneumatic tools are powered by compressed air and include chippers, drills, hammers, and sanders.

There are several dangers associated with the use of pneumatic tools. First and foremost is the danger of getting hit by one of the tool's attachments or by some kind of fastener the worker is using with the tool.

Pneumatic tools must be checked to see that the tools are fastened securely to the air hose to prevent them from becoming disconnected. A short wire or positive locking device attaching the air hose to the tool must also be used and will serve as an added safeguard.

If an air hose is more than $^1/_2$-inch (12.7 millimeters) in diameter, a safety excess flow valve must be installed at the source of the air supply to reduce pressure in case of hose failure.

In general, the same precautions should be taken with an air hose that are recommended for electric cords, because the hose is subject to the same kind of damage or accidental striking, and because it also presents tripping hazards.

When using pneumatic tools, a safety clip or retainer must be installed to prevent attachments such as chisels on a chipping hammer from being ejected during tool operation.

Pneumatic tools that shoot nails, rivets, staples, or similar fasteners and operate at pressures more than 100 pounds per square inch (6,890 kPa), must be equipped with a special device to keep fasteners from being ejected, unless the muzzle is pressed against the work surface.

Airless spray guns that atomize paints and fluids at pressures of 1,000 pounds or more per square inch (6,890 kPa) must be equipped with automatic or visible manual safety devices that will prevent pulling the trigger until the safety device is manually released.

Eye protection is required, and head and face protection is recommended for employees working with pneumatic tools.

Screens must also be set up to protect nearby workers from being struck by flying fragments around chippers, riveting guns, staplers, or air drills.

Compressed air guns should never be pointed toward anyone. Workers should never "dead-end" them against themselves or anyone else. A chip guard must be used when compressed air is used for cleaning.

Use of heavy jackhammers can cause fatigue and strains. Heavy rubber grips reduce these effects by providing a secure handhold. Workers operating a jackhammer must wear safety glasses and safety shoes that protect them against injury if the jackhammer slips or falls. A face shield also should be used.

Noise is another hazard associated with pneumatic tools. Working with noisy tools such as jackhammers requires proper, effective use of appropriate hearing protection.

Liquid Fuel Tools

Fuel-powered tools are usually operated with gasoline. The most serious hazard associated with the use of fuel-powered tools comes from fuel vapors that can burn or explode and also give off dangerous exhaust fumes. The worker must be careful to handle, transport, and store gas or fuel only in approved flammable liquid containers, according to proper procedures for flammable liquids.

Before refilling a fuel-powered tool tank, the user must shut down the engine and allow it to cool to prevent accidental ignition of hazardous vapors. When a fuel-powered tool is used inside a closed area, effective ventilation and/or proper respirators such as atmosphere-supplying respirators must be utilized to avoid breathing carbon monoxide. Fire extinguishers must also be available in the area.

Powder-Actuated Tools

Powder-actuated tools operate like a loaded gun and must be treated with extreme caution. In fact, they are so dangerous that they must be operated only by specially trained employees.

When using powder-actuated tools, an employee must wear suitable ear, eye, and face protection. The user must select a powder level—high or low velocity—that is appropriate for the powder-actuated tool and necessary to do the work without excessive force.

The muzzle end of the tool must have a protective shield or guard centered perpendicular to and concentric with the barrel to confine any fragments or particles that are projected when the tool is fired. A tool containing a high-velocity load must be designed not to fire unless it has this kind of safety device.

To prevent the tool from firing accidentally, two separate motions are required for firing. The first motion is to bring the tool into the firing position, and the second motion is to pull the trigger. The tool must not be able to operate until it is pressed against the work surface with a force of at least 5 pounds (2.2 kg) greater than the total weight of the tool.

If a powder-actuated tool misfires, the user must hold the tool in the operating position for at least 30 seconds before trying to fire it again. If it still will not fire, the user must hold the tool in the operating position for another 30 seconds and then carefully remove the load in accordance with the manufacturer's instructions. This procedure will make the faulty cartridge less likely to explode. The bad cartridge should then be put in water immediately after removal. If the tool develops a defect during use, it should be *tagged* and must be *taken out of service immediately* until it is properly repaired.

Safety precautions that must be followed when using powder-actuated tools include the following:

- Do not use a tool in an explosive or flammable atmosphere.
- Inspect the tool before using it to determine that it is clean, that all moving parts operate freely, and that the barrel is free from obstructions and has the proper shield, guard, and attachments recommended by the manufacturer.
- Do not load the tool unless it is to be used immediately.
- Do not leave a loaded tool unattended, especially where it would be available to unauthorized persons.
- Keep hands clear of the barrel end.
- Never point the tool at anyone.

When using powder-actuated tools to apply fasteners, several additional procedures must be followed:

- Do not fire fasteners into material that would allow the fasteners to pass through to the other side.
- Do not drive fasteners into very hard or brittle material that might chip or splatter or make the fasteners ricochet.
- Always use an alignment guide when shooting fasteners into existing holes.
- When using a high-velocity tool, do not drive fasteners more than 3 inches (7.62 centimeters) from an unsupported edge or corner of material such as brick or concrete.
- When using a high velocity tool, do not place fasteners in steel any closer than $1/2$-inch (1.27 centimeters) from an unsupported corner edge unless a special guard, fixture, or jig is used.

Hydraulic Power Tools

The fluid used in hydraulic power tools must be an approved fire-resistant fluid and must retain its operating characteristics at the most extreme temperatures to which it will be exposed. The exception to fire-resistant fluid involves all hydraulic fluids used for the insulated sections of derrick trucks, aerial lifts, and hydraulic tools that are used on or around energized lines. This hydraulic fluid shall be of the insulating type.

The manufacturer's recommended safe operating pressure for hoses, valves, pipes, filters, and other fittings must not be exceeded.

All jacks—including lever and ratchet jacks, screw jacks, and hydraulic jacks—must have a stop indicator, and the stop limit must not be exceeded. Also, the manufacturer's load limit must be permanently marked in a prominent place on the jack, and the load limit must not be exceeded.

A jack should never be used to support a lifted load. Once the load has been lifted, it must immediately be blocked up. Put a block under the base of the jack when the foundation is not firm, and place a block between the jack cap and load if the cap might slip.

To set up a jack, make certain of the following:

- The base of the jack rests on a firm, level surface;
- The jack is correctly centered;
- The jack head bears against a level surface; and
- The lift force is applied evenly.

Proper maintenance of jacks is essential for safety. All jacks must be lubricated regularly. In addition, each jack must be inspected according to the following schedule: (1) for jacks used continuously or intermittently at one site—inspected at least once every 6 months, (2) for jacks sent out of the shop for special work— inspected when sent out and inspected when returned, and (3) for jacks subjected to abnormal loads or shock—inspected before use and immediately thereafter.

OSHA can provide extensive help through a variety of programs, including assistance about safety and health programs, state plans, workplace consultations, voluntary protection programs, strategic partnerships, training and education, and more.

Safety and Health Program Management Guidelines

Working in a safe and healthful environment can stimulate innovation and creativity and result in increased performance and higher productivity.

To assist employers and employees in developing effective safety and health management systems, OSHA published recommended *Safety and Health Program Management Guidelines (Federal Register* 54(16): 3904-3916, January 26, 1989). These voluntary guidelines can be applied to all places of employment covered by OSHA.

The guidelines identify four general elements that are critical to the development of a successful safety and health management system. These are the following:

- Management leadership and employee involvement,
- Worksite analysis,
- Hazard prevention and control, and
- Safety and health training.

The guidelines recommend specific actions, under each of these general elements, to achieve an effective safety and health management system. The *Federal Register* notice is available online at www.osha.gov.

State Programs

The *Occupational Safety and Health Act of 1970 (OSH Act)* encourages states to develop and operate their own job safety and health plans. OSHA approves and monitors these plans. There are currently 26 state plans: 23 cover both private and public (state and local government) employment; 3 states, Connecticut, New Jersey, and New York, cover the public sector only. States and territories with their own OSHA-approved occupational safety and health plans must adopt and enforce standards identical to, or at least as effective as, the federal standards and provide extensive programs of voluntary compliance and technical assistance, including consultation services.

Consultation Services

Consultation assistance is available on request to employers who want help in establishing and maintaining a safe and healthful workplace. Largely funded by OSHA, the service is provided at no cost to the employer. Primarily developed for smaller employers with more hazardous operations, the consultation service is delivered by state governments employing professional safety and health consultants. Comprehensive assistance includes a hazard survey of the worksite and appraisal of all aspects of the employer's existing safety and health management system. In addition, the service offers assistance to employers in developing and implementing an effective safety and health management system. No penalties are proposed or citations issued for hazards identified by the consultant. The employer's only obligation is to correct all identified serious hazards within the agreed upon correction timeframe. OSHA provides consultation assistance to the employer with the assurance that his or her name and firm and any information about the workplace will not be routinely reported to OSHA enforcement staff.

Under the consultation program, certain exemplary employers may request participation in OSHA's Safety and Health Achievement Recognition Program (SHARP). Eligibility for participation in SHARP includes, but is not limited to, receiving a full-service, comprehensive consultation visit, correcting all identified hazards, and developing an effective safety and health program management system.

Employers accepted into SHARP may receive an exemption from programmed inspections (not complaint or accident investigation inspections) for a period of 1 year initially, or 2 years upon renewal. For more information concerning consultation assistance, see the list of consultation projects listed at the end of this publication.

Voluntary Protection Programs (VPP)

Voluntary Protection Programs and onsite consultation services, when coupled with an effective enforcement program, expand worker protection to help meet the goals of the *OSH Act*. The three levels of VPP—Star, Merit, and Demonstration—are designed to recognize outstanding achievements by companies that have developed and implemented effective safety and health management systems. The VPPs motivate others to achieve excellent safety and health results in the same outstanding way as they establish a cooperative relationship between employers, employees, and OSHA.

For additional information on VPPs and how to apply, contact the OSHA regional offices listed at the end of this publication.

Strategic Partnership Program

OSHA's Strategic Partnership Program, the newest member of OSHA's cooperative programs, helps encourage, assist, and recognize the efforts of partners to eliminate serious workplace hazards and achieve a high level of worker safety and health. Whereas OSHA's Consultation Program and VPP entail one-on-one relationships between OSHA and individual worksites, most strategic partnerships seek to have a broader impact by building cooperative relationships with groups of employers and employees. These partnerships are voluntary, cooperative relationships between OSHA, employers, employee representatives, and others such as trade unions, trade and professional associations, universities, and other government agencies.

For more information on this program, contact your nearest OSHA office, or visit OSHA's website at www.csha.gov.

Training and Education

OSHA's area offices offer a variety of information services, such as compliance assistance, technical advice, publications, audiovisual aids, and speakers for special engagements. OSHA's Training Institute in Des Plaines, IL, provides basic and advanced courses in safety and health for federal and state compliance officers, state consultants, federal agency personnel, and private sector employers, employees, and their representatives.

The OSHA Training Institute also has established OSHA Training Institute Education Centers to address the increased demand for its courses from the private sector and from other federal agencies. These centers are nonprofit colleges, universities, and other organizations that have been selected after a competition for participation in the program.

OSHA awards grants through its Susan Harwood Training Grant Program to nonprofit organizations to provide safety and health training and education to employers and workers in the workplace. The grants focus on programs that will educate workers and employers in small business (fewer than 250 employees), training workers and employers about new OSHA standards or about high-risk activities or hazards. Grants are awarded for 1 year and may be renewed for an additional 12-month period depending on whether the grantee has performed satisfactorily.

OSHA expects each organization awarded a grant to develop a training and/or education program that addresses a safety and health topic named by OSHA, recruit workers and employers for the training, and conduct the training. Grantees are also expected to follow up with people who have been trained to find out what changes were made to reduce the hazards in their workplaces as a result of the training.

Each year OSHA has a national competition that is announced in the *Federal Register* and on the Internet at www.osha-slc.gov/Training/sharwood/sharwood.html. For more information on grants, training, and education, contact the OSHA Training Institute, Office of Training and Education, 1555 Times Drive, Des Plaines, IL 60018; call (847) 297-4810, or see **Outreach** on OSHA's website at www.osha.gov.

Electronic Information

OSHA has a variety of materials and tools available on its website at www.osha.gov. These include e-Tools, Expert Advisors, Electronic Compliance Assistance Tools (e-CATs), Technical Links, regulations, directives, publications, videos, and other information for employers and employees. OSHA's software programs and compliance assistance tools "walk" you through challenging safety and health issues and common problems to find the best solutions for your workplace.

OSHA's CD-ROM includes standards, interpretations, directives, and more and can be purchased on CD-ROM from the U.S. Government Printing Office. To order, write to the Superintendent of Documents, U.S. Government Printing Office, Washington, DC 20402, or phone (202) 512-1800. Specify OSHA Regulations, Documents and Technical Information on CD-ROM (ORDT), GPO Order No. S/N 729-013-00000-5. The price is $45 per year ($63.00 overseas); $21 per single copy ($26.25 overseas).

OSHA Publications

OSHA has an extensive publications program. For a listing of free or sales items, visit OSHA's website at www.osha.gov or contact the OSHA Publications Office , U.S. Department of Labor, OSHA/OSHA Publications, PO Box 37535, Washington, DC 20013-7535. Telephone (202) 693-1888 or fax to (202) 693-2498.

All About OSHA - OSHA 2056

Chemical Hazard Communication - OSHA 3084

Controlling Electrical Hazards - OSHA 3075

Ground Fault Protection on Construction Sites - OSHA 3007

Hearing Conservation - OSHA 3074

The following publications are available from the Superintendent of Documents, U.S. Government Printing Office, Washington, DC 20402, telephone (202) 512-1800, fax (202) 512-2250. Include the GPO order number and make checks payable to the Superintendent of Documents. Visa or MasterCard are accepted.

Hazard Communication - A Compliance Kit (OSHA 3104),

GPO Order No. 929-016-00200-6, $20.00 ($25.00 overseas).

Hazard Communication - Guidelines for Compliance (OSHA 3111)

Order No. 029-016-00195-6. $4.25 ($5.31 overseas).

Job Safety and Health Quarterly magazine, GPO Order Processing Code #JSH, annual subscription $17.00 ($21.25 foreign; single copies, $6.00 ($7.50 foreign). Order from the U.S. Government Printing Office, Superintendent of Documents, Washington, DC 20402, Fax (202)512-2233.

Emergencies, Complaints, and Further Assistance

To report an emergency, file a complaint, or seek OSHA advice, assistance, or products, call (800) 321-OSHA or contact your nearest OSHA regional, area, state plan, or consultation office listed at the end of this publication. The teletypewriter (TTY) number is (877) 889-5627.

You can also file a complaint online and obtain more information on OSHA federal and state programs by visiting OSHA's website at www.osha.gov.

Commissioner
Alaska Department of Labor
1111 West 8th Street
Room 304
Juneau, AK 99801-1149
(907) 465-2700

Director
Industrial Comm. of Arizona
800 W. Washington
Phoenix, AZ 85007-2922
(602) 542-5795

Director
California Department of
  Industrial Relations
455 Golden Gate Avenue
10th Floor
San Francisco, CA 94102
(415) 703-5050

Commissioner
Connecticut Departmentof Labor
200 Folly Brook Boulevard
Wethersfield, CT 06109
(203) 566-5123

Director
Hawaii Department of Labor
  and Industrial Relations
830 Punchbowl Street
Honolulu, HI 96813
(808) 586-8844

Commissioner
Indiana Department of Labor
State Office Building
402 West Washington Street
Room W195
Indianapolis, IN 46204-2751
(317) 232-2378

Commissioner
Iowa Division of Labor Services
1000 E. Grand Avenue
Des Moines, IA 50319-0209
(515) 281-3447

Secretary
Kentucky Labor Cabinet
1049 U.S. Highway, 127 South
Suite 4
Frankfort, KY 40601
(502) 564-3070

Commissioner
Maryland Division of Labor
  and Industry
Department of Labor, Licensing,
  and Regulation
1100 N. Eutaw Street, Room 613
Baltimore, MD 21201-2206
(410) 767-2215

Director
Michigan Department of
  Consumer and Industry Services
P.O. Box 30004
4th Floor, Law Building
Lansing, MI 48909
(517) 373-7230

Commissioner
Minnesota Department of Labor
and Industry
443 Lafayette Road
St. Paul, MN 55155-4307
(651) 296-2342

Administrator
Nevada Division of Industrial
Relations
400 West King Street
Carson City, NV 89710
(775) 687-3032

Commissioner
New Jersey Department
of Labor
John Fitch Plaza
Market and Warren Streets
P.O. Box 110
Trenten, NJ 08625-0110
(609) 292-2975

Secretary
New Mexico Environment
Department
1190 St. Francis Drive
P.O. Box 26110
Santa Fe, NM 87502
(505) 827-2850

Commissioner
New York Department of Labor
W. Averell Harriman State
Office Building - 12
Room 500
Albany, NY 12240
(518) 457-2741

Commissioner
North Carolina Department
of Labor
4 West Edenton Street
Raleigh, NC 27601-1092
(919) 807-2900

Administrator
Department of Consumer
and Business Services
Occupational Safety and Health
Division (OR-OSHA)
350 Winter Street, NE
Room 430
Salem, OR 97310-0220
(503) 378-3272

Secretary
Puerto Rico Department of Labor
and Human Resources
Prudencio Rivera Martinez
Building
505 Munoz Rivera Avenue
Hato Rey, PR 00918
(787) 754-2119

Director
South Carolina Department of
Labor, Licensing, and Regulation
Koger Office Park,
Kingstree Building
110 Centerview Drive
P.O. Box 11329
Columbia, SC 29210
(803) 896-4300

Commissioner
Tennessee Department of Labor
710 James Robertson Parkway
Nashville, TN 37243-0659
(615) 741-2582

Commissioner
Labor Commission of Utah
160 East 300 South, 3rd Floor
P.O. Box 146650
Salt Lake City, UT 84114-6650
(801) 530-6898

Commissioner
Vermont Department of Labor
and Industry
National Life Building
Drawer 20
National Life Drive
Montpelier, VT 05260-3401
(802) 828-5098

State	Telephone
Alabama	(205) 348-3033
Alaska	(907) 269-4957
Arizona	(602) 542-1695
Arkansas	(501) 682-4522
California	(916) 574-2555
Colorado	(970) 491-6151
Connecticut	(860) 566-4550
Delaware	(302) 761-8219
District of Columbia	(202) 541-3727
Florida	(813) 974-9962
Georgia	(404) 894-2643
Guam	9-1-(671) 475-0136
Hawaii	(808) 586-9100
Idaho	(208) 426-3283
Illinois	(312) 814-2337
Indiana	(317) 232-2688
Iowa	(515) 281-7629
Kansas	(785) 296-7476
Kentucky	(502) 564-6895
Louisiana	(225) 342-9601
Maine	(207) 624-6460
Maryland	(410) 880-4970
Massachusetts	(617) 727-3982
Michigan	(517) 322-6823
Minnesota	(651) 297-2393
Mississippi	(601) 987-3981
Missouri	(573) 751-3403
Montana	(406) 444-6418
Nebraska	(402) 471-4717
Nevada	(702) 486-9140
New Hampshire	(603) 271-2024
New Jersey	(609) 292-3923
New Mexico	(505) 827-4230
New York	(518) 457-2238
North Carolina	(919) 807-2905
North Dakota	(701) 328-5188
Ohio	(614) 644-2246
Oklahoma	(405) 528-1500
Oregon	(503) 378-3272
Pennsylvania	(724) 357-2396

Puerto Rico ....(787) 754-2171
Rhode Island ....(401) 222-2438
South Carolina ....(803) 734-9614
South Dakota ....(605) 688-4101
Tennessee ....(615) 741-7036
Texas ....(512) 804-4640
Utah ....(801) 530-6901
Vermont ....(802) 828-2765
Virginia ....(804) 786-6359
Virgin Islands..(809) 772-1315
Washington ....(360) 902-5638
West Virginia ....(304) 558-7890
Wisconsin ....(608) 266-8579
Wyoming ....(307) 777-7786

Area	Telephone
Birmingham, AL	(205) 731-1534
Mobile, AL	(334) 441-6131
Anchorage, AK	(907) 271-5152
Phoenix, AZ	(602) 640-2348
Little Rock, AR	(501) 324-6291(5818)
San Diego, CA	(619) 557-5909
Sacramento, CA	(916) 566-7471
Denver, CO	(303) 844-5285
Englewood, CO	(303) 843-4500
Bridgeport, CT	(203) 579-5581
Hartford, CT	(860) 240-3152
Wilmington, DE	(302) 573-6518
Fort Lauderdale, FL	(954) 424-0242
Jacksonville, FL	(904) 232-2895
Tampa, FL	(813) 626-1177
Savannah, GA	(912) 652-4393
Smyrna, GA	(770) 984-8700
Tucker, GA	(770) 493-6644/6742/8419
Boise, ID	(208) 321-2960
Calumet City, IL	(708) 891-3800
Des Plaines, IL	(847) 803-4800
Fairview Heights, IL	(618) 632-8612
North Aurora, IL	(630) 896-8700
Peoria, IL	(309) 671-7033
Indianapolis, IN	(317) 226-7290
Des Moines, IA	(515) 284-4794
Wichita, KS	(316) 269-6644
Frankfort, KY	(502) 227-7024
Baton Rouge, LA	(225) 389-0474 (0431)
Bangor, ME	(207) 941-8177
Portland, ME	(207) 780-3178
August, ME	(207) 622-8417
Linthicum, MD	(410) 865-2055/2056
Braintree, MA	(617) 565-6924
Methuen, MA	(617) 565-8110
Springfield, MA	(413) 785-0123
Lansing, MI	(517) 327-0904
Minneapolis, MN	(612) 664- 5460
Jackson, MS	(601) 965-4606
Kansas City, MO	(816) 483-9531

Area	Telephone
St. Louis, MO	(314) 425-4289
Billings, MT	(406) 247-7494
Raleigh, NC	(919) 856-4770
Omaha, NE	(402) 221-3182
Carson City, NV	(775) 885-6963
Concord, NH	(603) 225-1629
Avenel, NJ	(732) 750-3270
Hasbrouck Heights, NJ	(201) 288-1700
Marlton, NJ	(609) 757-5181
Parsippany, NJ	(973) 263-1003
Albuquerque, NM	(505) 248-5302
Albany, NY	(518) 464-4338
Bayside, NY	(718) 279-9060
Bowmansville, NY	(716) 684-3891
North Syracuse, NY	(315) 451-0808
Tarrytown, NY	(914) 524-7510
Westbury, NY	(516) 334-3344
Bismark, ND	(701) 250-4521
Cincinnati, OH	(513) 841-4132
Cleveland, OH	(216) 522-3818
Columbus, OH	(614) 469-5582
Toledo, OH	(419) 259-7542
Oklahoma City, OK	(405) 231-5351(5389)
Portland, OR	(503) 326-2251
Allentown, PA	(610) 776-0592
Erie, PA	(814) 833-5758
Harrisburg, PA	(717) 782-3902
Philadelphia, PA	(215) 597-4955
Pittsburgh, PA	(412) 395-4903
Wilkes-Barre, PA	(570) 826-6538
Guaynabo, PR	(787) 277-1560
Providence, RI	(401) 528-4669
Columbia, SC	(803) 765-5904
Nashville, TN	(615) 781-5423
Austin, TX	(512) 916-5783 (5788)
Corpus Christi, TX	(512) 888-3420
Dallas, TX	(214) 320-2400 (2558)
El Paso, TX	(915) 534-6251
Fort Worth, TX	(817) 428-2470 (485-7647)
Houston, TX	(281) 591-2438 (2787)

Area	Telephone
Houston, TX	(281) 286-0583/0584 (5922)
Lubbock, TX	(806) 472-7681 (7685)
Salt Lake City, UT	(801) 530-6901
Norfolk, VA	(757) 441-3820
Bellevue, WA	(206) 553-7520
Charleston, WV	(304) 347-5937
Appleton, WI	(920) 734-4521
Eau Claire, WI	(715) 832-9019
Madison, WI	(608) 264-5388
Milwaukee, WI	(414) 297-3315

Region I
(CT,* MA, ME, NH, RI, VT*)
JFK Federal Building
Room E-340
Boston, MA 02203
Telephone: (617) 565-9860

Region II
(NJ,* NY,* PR,* VI*)
201 Varick Street
Room 670
New York, NY 10014
Telephone: (212) 337-2378

Region III
(DC, DE, MD,* PA, VA,* WV)
The Curtis Center - Suite 740 West
170 S. Independence Mall West
Philadelphia, PA 19106-3309
Telephone: (215) 861-4900

Region IV
(AL, FL, GA. KY,* MS, NC,* SC,* TN*)
Atlanta Federal Center
61 Forsyth Street, SW, Room 6T50
Atlanta, GA 30303
Telephone: (404) 562-2300

Region V
(IL, IN,* MI,* MN,* OH, WI)
230 South Dearborn Street
Room 3244
Chicago, IL 60604
Telephone: (312) 353-2220

Region VI
(AR, LA, MN,* OK, TX)
525 Griffin Street
Room 602
Dallas, TX 75202
Telephone: (214) 767-4731

Region VII
(IA,* KS, MO, NE)
City Center Square
1100 Main Street, Suite 800
Kansas City, MO 64105
Telephone: (816) 426-5861

Region VIII
(CO, MT, ND, SD, UT,* WY*)
1999 Broadway
Suite 1690
Denver, CO 80802-5716
Telephone: (303) 844-1600

Region IX
(American Samoa, AZ,* CA,* Guam, HI,* NV,* Commonwealth of the Northern Mariana Islands)
71 Stevenson Street
4th Floor
San Francisco, CA 94105
Telephone: (415) 975-4310

Region X
(AK,* ID, OR,* WA*)
1111 Third Avenue
Suite 715
Seattle, WA 98101-3212
Telephone: (206) 553-5930

*These states and territories operate their own OSHA-approved job safety and health programs (Connecticut, New Jersey, and New York plans cover public employees only). States with approved programs must have a standard that is identical to, or at least as effective as, the federal standard.